Introduction

Passive income is an interesting topic that is worth to explore. Many people are attracted to this topic. I hope you are one of these cool people. Now let's dive in with me.

Chapter 1: What exactly passive income is

The words passive income close to you day by day than you think, but it is very hard to work or achieve something if you are not sure what it really is. If you want to earn passive income, first you need to know the true definition of passive income.

Passive income and active income

Passive income is the money or revenue that still run into your pocket when you are not working. It is good because you earn money without working physically and mentally. Some people prefer another name of passive income that is residual income.

Opposite with passive income, you have to work and earn money. You either pay by hours or base salary each month. This type is calling active income. With active income, you have to work physically or mentally to earn the money.

Active income is good too. However, you will have to work to earn money. If you stop working, the money will stop also. Many reasons for stop earning active income may happen such as you quit your daily job, you got fired from your job, the company or organization laid people off or close its business.

These incidents may happen, and we hear a lot from our friends and family, the news. When the incident happens, you may or may not receive supporting money from the company.

Passive Income

The True Definition and 10 Awesome Ideas to Make $10,000 Each Month

© Copyright 2018 by Noah Gladwyn -All rights reserved.

Author reserve all rights to this document. No one is allowed to print, reproduce, copy or mimic any of the passage of this document without written permission of the author. Reviewers are allowed to quote a few lines in the reviews.

Disclaimer

No section, line or paragraph of the publication must be reproduced and transmitted by mechanical, electronic or handwriting mean, such as photocopy, recording or any other system without permission in writing from author and publisher.

The purpose of this document is to share verified information, but the author and publisher will not assume any liability for errors, omission and opposing interoperations of the content herein.

The purpose of this book is entertainment and the views and ideas in the book only belong to the author. These ideas should not be taken as expert advice and commands. The readers are only responsible for their actions for doing anything wrong after reading this book.

Only purchaser and reader are responsible to adhere to the application of laws and regulations in their state for advertising, professional licensing and business practices.

Neither author nor the publisher will assume responsibility or liability for actions of purchaser or reader. All brands and trademarks in this book are for clarification purposes and owned by the owners only. They are not affiliated with the document.

Table of Content

Introduction..5
Chapter 1: What exactly passive income is...............................6
Chapter 2: Blogging and passive income................................ 11
Chapter 3: Graphic t-shirts design and passive income........... 15
Chapter 4: Trading Cryptocurrency and passive income........ 20
Chapter 5: Selling your professional photos online and passive income..24
Chapter 6: Developing phone apps and passive income......... 30
Chapter 7: Writing online reviews and passive income........... 35
Chapter 8: Get paid for lending money on credible platforms and passive income..39
Chapter 9: Get Paid to search and evaluate on the internet and passive income..41
Chapter 10: Cash back credit cards and passive income..........44
Chapter 11: Use your expertise and passive income................ 47
Conclusion.. 49

If you receive supporting or severance money, you will only receive it for certain period of time. Then you will have to look for the new job or new opportunity.

Besides that, active income is also earned by contract job. In the contract job, you still have to work to earn your money. Contract job is a little bit more flexible in working time. However, you stop working or the contract is expired, then you will not earn any money.

What good about passive income

With these reasons are mentioned above, passive income often seems like a better choice. You will get money rolling in your bank account although you do not work. That is not mean you will not work at all or you just sign up or apply something, and you will get paid.

At first, you will have to set up your business or your passive income stream. When starting up, you will have to do quite amount of work to get your passive income stream or business to rolling.

Your business or passive income stream will keep increase and reach to passive income point. This is a crucial point to get. The passive income will come to you. You can decide to continue to work or work less or even not over certain period of time.

At this time, it doesn't matter because you earn money any way. You should not mistake passive income with the big chunk of money that you receive at one time. Passive income is the income that you receive continually even time come by.

Is passive income perfect?

I just want to make sure that passive income is not running or lasting forever. Finally, everything will run out, and passive income is also not the exception. It will run out at the end because of different factors.

Each passive income stream or business is different from each other. It depends on what type and model of the streams and business. Some passive income streams or business will run for couple years. Some may run for longer time such as decades or centuries.

The risk is also the big factor on your passive income stream. Risk is always appearing in any form of business that generate income. You will never have 100% full security because there will always the risk involved.

You can do as best as you can to maintenance your passive income stream. You can minimize the risks if you maintenance your business the right way. One of the best way is creating or having multiple passive income streams. They are will reduce the risks many time.

You should decide the certain time that you will care and support your passive income streams. Passive income stream or business needs to be maintenance like any other business. However, you will do just decent things such as checking mails or emails, keep track with the checks, money and basic accounting, etc.

You still have to report and file income tax with your passive income stream. This is important, and you should always remember to do it on time. You do not want that your passive income streams would be in tax trouble.

Passive income streams are different. Some streams are very passive, but some streams are not totally passive. For example, if you write books and post in the platform to sell, you will not have a lot of works to do. All you need to do is checking for your royalties because the platform take care of everything that is from selling your books to dealing with customers.

Another example is about passive income but it is not totally passive and needed some works to be done. This example is that you have houses and you want to rent them out.

This is a good passive income stream because you will collect the payment from your tenants. However, you will also have to spend time and effort to keep up this passive income stream.

You will do things such as pay property taxes, pay insurances for the house, background checking the tenants, improve and maintain you houses, find the tenants to fill up the vacancy, etc. You may have somebody working for you, but you still want to be on top of everything in your business.

As we see, passive income is not for everybody. Some people will do work for active income. You will have to set up your business to passive income if you really want this income stream. Nowadays technologies are also very helpful for passive income purpose.

Passive income streams are a really business that you will have to work hard to achieve. They are never the get rich quick schemes. You must provide for your customers or your audiences the real value. That will help your business stay and become better for the long time. Then the result is the passive income stream.

Chapter 2: Blogging and passive income

After you know the true definition of passive income, you can see this is really an interesting way of financial freedom. Here is one of the ways that you can earn passive income stream is blogging.

What is good about blogging?

You can create a blog easily nowadays. You can work at home with blogging. When you work at home, the schedule will be more flexible. It is completely different schedule compare to other traditional jobs. You will have flexible time to spending with your love ones.

You will be the owner or the boss of your blog. At your own boss, you will earn more if you work with the right strategies. You will decide the time that you are working. With the good blog, you can earn passive income even when you sleep or on your traveling vacation.

The reason is the content of your blog is available all the time on the platform or service. Your audiences can come and check out whenever they want. You do not have to stay up all the time to open your blog for your audiences to come like tradition jobs.

Passive income stream from blogging is working to keep up your blog. You will receive the income from your content or past content also. Like I mentioned above, you can make money even when you are sleeping. However, you still need to put time and effort in your blogging career.

Ways to earn money with blogging

Content of your blog is so important. You will need the valuable and relevant content to build up your audiences or followers. You can promote relevant services or products by putting the affiliate links in your content.

This a good way to earn passive income. Your audiences or followers will see your content. They will decide to purchase the products or service or not. You do not have to do anything besides putting the affiliate links.

When you write your content all the time, your writing skill will get sharp. You can write couple books or ebooks and post on popular platforms to earn some good royalties. This is ways for you to using your skills in different aspect.

You will become better and more professional blogger by time and the effort that you dedicate for your business. You can create a course or dedicate a part of your blog to teaching people how to be a blogger and earn extra money.

These above things are just one of many ways to make passive income with your blog. As you see, you still have to put in the work. However, your skills and the ways that you set up your business will bring the money even when you take a short break.

If you love blogging, you will enjoy doing it. You will not see it like a duty that you have to get through to earn money. You will find the way to automate certain parts of your business. You will focus more on which things you believe that can scale up your blog faster.

Use your blog to provide value and have right strategies to monetize your audiences

You can have passive income ways with your blog. You build the trust level with your audiences through blogging. It will be easier for you to have the landing pages to collect audiences' email addresses. Now you can contact with them through email

You can email your audiences to offer the free sample of relevant products or services that they already want to look for. You send them in certain time within 4 or 7 days. In each sending email, you should also put the affiliate links. Not all of your audiences will buy, but some of them will buy. You earn passive income thorough these commission.

Next, you can do similar with your books or ebooks. You have the skills to write the content with the special niche that you pick for your blog. You will have the books or ebooks that offer your audiences.

Besides having your ebooks on popular platforms, you can promote them as well through your blog or email. You should make sure that your ebooks provide valuable content that audiences are looking for.

Blogging also helps you with the create step by step skills. You can take that advantage to create your own relevant online courses. If you provide good value and know how to market it right in your blog and email to the audiences. It will make you good passive income as well. That is said blogging is really a good passive income stream.

Chapter 3: Graphic t-shirts design and passive income

Blogging is a good way to have passive income, but it is not the only way. Next, we will explore another opportunity that is selling t-shirts design. This way is relating more to the physical products side.

Advantages of selling t-shirts design

Selling t-shirts design has been easier than ever. You have the fulfillment companies or special platforms that help you handle a lot of complicated processes such as printing the t-shirts, receiving the orders, handle the shipping, etc.

In addition, you will do not need a lot of money to invest or most of the time is no money that is required at all. You can manage to get into this business easily. Many companies are do drop shipping for your t-shirts or products.

With drop shipping service in selling t-shirts design, it is a little bit different. You can just focus to create your t-shirts design. The manufactures will take care the rest of the process for you. However, when the customers receive the t-shirts, all of the transaction will be on your business website.

Like other business, selling t-shirts design need time and effort too. It is not another get rich quick scheme. You will need use the right strategies to run your business. You also need to promote your t-shirts design to the potential customers.

You can earn good passive income with this business if you commit to it. Many people will wear your t-shirts design, and you make pretty nice passive income as the same time. It sounds awesome, isn't it?

Build your online store

Having an online store for your products or t-shirts design is a good idea. You will have a firm online presence. Many of platforms or services will provide the online store website for you.

You just need to do some quick research and pick the right one for your business. Some things you should keep in mind when picking the right services such as monthly fee, is it easy to use, easy to customize, incorporate well with other input software, etc.

The popular platforms for e-commerce and drop shipping are Shopify, LemonStand, BigCommerce, etc. After you pick a platform, you should start to play around and custom your online store in the way that will attract customers to visit.

After you pick the platform and build your online store on, you will need to do another diligent research for the fulfillment company. You will have to make sure the fulfillment company integrate well with your online store.

Ways to deal with customers

You have the fulfillment company that helps you to delivery the t-shirts design. However, it is your responsibility to deal with your customers. You will have to create the full or almost comprehensive customer service pages.

These pages should include frequently asked questions, refund policies, your contact information that customers can reach you, etc. These are really important because they show to the customers that you have a legit business and are willing be here to help and serve.

Create t-shirts design

This process is the important and exciting part in the business. You will first brainstorm a lot of ideas to create the unique t-shirts design. You should write those ideas down. Then you need to download the template that is required by the printing company.

The printing company will have certain guidelines for you to follow such as sizes, colors, what types of uploading files, etc. The company want to make sure you are on the same page with it until the final products or t-shirts is completed and delivering to the customers.

You can either choose to design by yourself or outsource for other people to design for you. This step is up to you. If you want to do it on your own, many t-shirts design software or programs are available such as Adobe, Gimp, Canva, etc.

Upload t-shirts design

You will upload or send your designs to the fulfillment company. You will decide the sizes, colors that you want to offer in your online store. You will have to have a good communication back and forth. If you have any change, you will have to update right away with the fulfillment company.

Right way to price your t-shirts

When you work with the print fulfillment company, you do not have to pay anything upfront. When the orders are placed, you now pay. The company often charges you base price of the material and shipping cost.

You will have to add your own mark up if you want to get the profit from each t-shirt is sold. For example, from the fulfillment company that the base price of the t-shirt is $7, and the shipping cost is $3.

If you want to get the profit of $5, you will have to add up the price of the t-shirt is $12 and you still charge $3 for shipping cost. This is just an example. You have to consider about the quality of making the t-shirts.

You need to make sure to test the quality or choices out with your potential customers. When you want to scale up your business, you must provide what your customers want. In the end, they will be the ones to purchase your t-shirts.

Write a good description

Ever product or t-shirt needs a good description to catch attention of potential customers. You should describe what is about your design and what it mean.

You will need to write clearly about what types of the t-shirts and their material. You should include the size chart clearly. One more important thing is shipping time. You will show the customers the time that they will receive their t-shirts.

The good description will save you a lot of time later. Customers can get full information in the description. They will not send you emails or messages to ask you because the information is clear and helpful.

Chapter 4: Trading Cryptocurrency and passive income

The cryptocurrency is one of the hot topic of this year. It is a very interesting market for investors and traders. Besides that, cryptocurrency also has a very strong side to make a good passive income stream.

Cryptocurrencies in general

Bitcoin is the most popular cryptocurrency. The value of Bitcoin is increasing a lot last couple years until now. Just about five years, the value of Bitcoin increase more than hundred times.

This is pretty good for people who invest or trade in Bitcoin early. What a nice passive income stream. That is why the cryptocurrency market is very interesting to take a look at.

Beside Bitcoin, there are many different cryptocurrencies that are in the market right now. They may have big potential as well to give their users, investors or traders the high percent of return like Bitcoin does.

Trade for cryptocurrencies

You have to focus and research when you invest or trade cryptocurrencies. I know it is still a new trading market, but it is never simple and easy. It always requires discipline, good knowledge, patience and diligence up to date research.

You can see how Bitcoin increase in price. It is really an interesting but also very volatile marketplace. The risk are very high, but the return is super high too. You have to equip yourself with the right strategies to avoid bad choices when you trade.

Many people start to invest in other cryptocurrencies than Bitcoin. These crypcurrencies or coins are still cheap to buy now. They are also called altcoins. Some of them are Ethereum, Neo, Siacoin, Litecoin, etc.

Some of these altcoins have the potential to yield high return like Bitcoin. Many investors and traders are focusing on these altcoins right now. They don't want to miss another huge opportunity like before.

Prominent altcoins

A lot of new altcoins have potential to grow really quickly. Litecoin may be one of them. Litecoin have increase trade volume a lot in many exchange platform. The new traders are interested in Litecoin as well.

The trading for Litecoin is easy to happen. The transaction is not complicated like other altcoins. It makes Litecoin are really favored over the other altcoins. The professional investors and hedge fund managers are trading quite large amount of Litecoin.

When Litecoin was first introduced for couple years, the value was stay still. You did not see a any increasing value. Just last year, Litecoin is increasing around 80 times. It is really increasing s lot.

Besides Litecoin, Ethereum is also increase value really quickly too. Ethereum give a good passive income for many early investors. Last year, Ethereum is increasing more than 90 times of its previous value.

Ripple is also one of the prominent altcoins. It is also increasing value quickly too. That is about more than 50%. Ripple is under observation of many investors or traders in the future.

What altcoins are worth

A lot of these altcoins are introducing to the marketplace. Some of them are valuable. Some of them are not. You need to do the good research to find out and pick the right one.

The experienced traders are always do their diligent research before they make the trade for any altcoins. They know that the gain and the loss are very close in this volatile market. Nobody wants to take a loss in the business.

Bitcoin is already established its place in the cryptocurrency world and continue growing. Now you will have to search for the right new altcoins, and you see these new altcoins may or may not have the potential growth.

Although you invest or trade in cryptocurrencies that can give you a nice passive income, you should take time to do the real work. The reason is that your own money. You put it in the market for the growth.

You will hear many kinds of opinion or advice from different people. You should take in your consideration. At the same time, you do your comprehensive research and check really closely where your money go into.

Cryptocurrency market will go up and down just like other traditional markets. If you do your research well, you will not be confused. You will have the clear mind to give the right strategies to adapt and make a growth in any market situation.

Chapter 5: Selling your professional photos online and passive income

If you have a passion to taking nice photos, this will be an awesome opportunity for passive income stream. You may still be the part time photographer, but now you can earn big potential of money doing what you love.

Benefits from your own website

Every passive income stream is needed work just like other business models. The cost of creating a website is not expensive anymore. If you are a photographer and you love this career, you should create your own website.

The website will give you many advantages. You can advertise your services to online world, potential customers will reach you easily. You can also present your previous works or past achievement awards on your website to increase your credibility in the field. The website can also help you integrate all of your social media accounts.

You have your own website. You can advertise your photographer service. How much price it is in each package. You can also sell your professional photos on your website. This is really good stream of income since your followers already interest in what you do.

You can also sell the licensed of your photos for stock photos. Many people really love your photos. They may want to get the licensed to using for their commercial purposes.

As you see, the income stream that you have by owning a website will be way higher than the fee of running the website. It is really a smart investment. Potential customers can make the purchase directly on your website.

In the past, the choice is very limited for photographers. If you are a photographer, you have only one option that was selling on stock website. You have to create or apply for your accounts.

You then upload your photos to them. You rely heavily on the third party. Stock websites will sell you photos and you earn your commission around 20% to 30%. They take a large portion of the profit from you

However, nowadays you can sell your photos on other new platforms. You can keep all of the profit. You can set up the price for your photos and what the niche you are strongly in. Many advantages are in these new platforms. You just need to do research to meet your own needs.

How to sell your photos

The demand for online photos or images are higher than ever. You go to the internet, and you will see many websites, blogs or platforms. They are all includes many of many pictures. The pictures are mostly stock photos.

With increasing of ebooks, the demand for digital stock photos are increasing as well. Many stock photo platforms was born to satisfy the needs of their customers. The customers are variety such as ebooks writers, designers, bloggers, business owners, online marketers, etc.

Customers will have the different demand for quality and licensed photos to using in their business. Stock photos online are using really in any aspect of life. These are examples as blog posts, website designs, newsletters, flyers, book covers, ebook covers, and many more.

At the photographer's viewpoint, you can make a really good passive income stream with these high demands for online photos. You just need to create a big collection of pictures. The market will really need them.

You can go to the popular stock photos platforms, and do a little bit research to see which types of photos get the most sales or downloaded. These photos are the ones you want to start and have in your collection or portfolio of photos.

Besides selling photos on your own website, you can sell them to other new stock photos platforms. These new platforms are better than the old ones in the past. They always improve their services. The popular ones are such as Shutterstock, Fotolia, iStock, etc.

The new stock photos platforms have many advantage. They can reach to hundred thousands of potential customers a day. They will have to market their business. Your photos will get promote by them.

Like I mentioned above, you will have to save some profit with the platforms. They often called service fees. However, the platforms will handle certain complicated processes for your photos business.

Different platforms offer different business deals with your photos. You will do research to see with ones that are good for you. Some platforms will set the price low so they can sell your photos in high volume. Some will sell your photos with high price. Then you get high royalties, but you get low volume sale.

Selling on your website

You will have more work to do when you sell the photos on your own website. However, you will get all of the money come from sale. You will be your own boss. You will be the one to decide how to run your business.

You will decide with collections or portfolio that you want to attract and deliver to your potential customers. You should build and collect huge photos for your business even from the beginning.

In the past, it was so complicated to own a website. The fees and costs are really high to run a website. However, it is way too simple to own a website now. You can easily set up the website for selling photos online with low costs or even free.

Many platforms that you can build your website on are available. WordPress is very popular to new people that want to build their own websites.

When you look for the specific platform for building website, you should make sure that it will have clear instructions about set up the site, convenient plugins such as protect passwords, process the payment faster, protect your photos, etc.

The platform is also easy to integrate all of your social media accounts to increase your website credibility to customers. You should start to selling photos and make money right away after you completely set up the website.

Now you make your own decision for the business. You need to have a deep research for the price that you want to sale. All of the profit will come to you. However, you will have to compete with big stock photo platforms.

You should price your photos a little lower than other competitors. You have to check on the market and your main competitors to stay relevant with your customers.

You will have to apply the right strategies for the business. You can create different collections depends on which topics that the customers want. You can also have a bundle or discount price in special events.

With selling on your own website, one of the biggest thing is that you can build your own brand in your photos business. It will take more time and effort when you first start it. You will need adapt and up to date within your community.

You should also have free photos that will put in free stock photo platforms. Then you have a link to come back to your own website. You will reach more potential customers this way. That is said when your brand is established, the income stream will just come in your pocket with way less work than before.

Chapter 6: Developing phone apps and passive income

This part will be related a lot in technology. You use and look at your smartphone many times a day. Is it interesting if you can develop an app and also receive the passive income at the same time?

Develop apps market

The app market is becoming bigger and more important everyday. There are apps that paid to use. The consumers are happy to purchase those awesome apps for their smartphones. A lot of potential money that are to be earned in this market are for sure.

You should read and learn about the coding in your free time. That knowledge is really useful for developing apps. Besides that, you also need the skills to understand what the market wants.

App stores

You have to be register to the app stores to allowing to create or develop an app. Many people use smartphones, and they always hear about these two app stores. These two biggest app stores are Apple App Store and Google Play Store.

These two app stores have their own requirements, but first you have to apply and get accept by them to become their member. You have to pay around $99 a year to active your membership as an app developer of Apple.

Apple will provide you tools to test. It has a team to check on your app to make sure that the app is good and meeting the requirements. After your app is done, it will get distribute to all of Apple devices such as iPhone, iPad, MacBook, etc.

Google Play charges way lesser fee. That is around $25 for only one time. It also provides test and useful tools for developers. Both app store are very popular to user. You will earn potential big passive income stream here. Every time users purchase or upgrade your apps. You will get pay.

What kind of app you want to develop

You need to have a clear plan about what you are going to develop. You cannot wait and say that you will figure it out later. It has to be at the beginning.

Same with creating any products or services, you will have to pick the right niche to start developing your app. The niche needs to have a good market or enough consumers are in.

You cannot pick the niche that nobody wants to purchase your app. You have to do the research on your competitors as well.

You need to see how well the competitors' apps are and how they price their apps in the niche.

Many popular apps are using this good strategy. These apps are often download for free by users. Then they have the upgrade versions that users will purchase because they love the apps.

You can see these examples are in app for games. These apps have certain free level that the free users can achieve. After playing the game for awhile, users pass all of the free levels. They still love the game, so they make the decision to purchase the upgrade version.

That is said your app must be high quality and provide what your customers want. You cannot develop the poor app for free in the beginning and expect your customers pay for the upgrade versions later.

Dealing with customers or users

When your app is available in the store, you will start the process to deal with the customers right away. This is a big part of the internet world. You will receive the reviews and feedback from users.

Some reviews and feedback are nice. The users give good expression about how good your app is. Some feedback will be hash and rude without any reason. That is just the nature of online business, you should not feel discourage.

In addition, some reviews and feedback are constructive. They are very helpful for you to take a look of your app in the different angles and fix the problems immediately. You will improve your app better for users.

You will respond to your users actively because users have the power to rate your app. You want to build the good relationship with them and receive highest rating stars as possible.

In this case, it is five stars reviews. When new users are interesting to download your app and they see five stars reviews, they will more like to download or purchase your app for their smartphone.

In your app, you should set up the portion of rating before users can leave the reviews an feedback. Many users just skim quickly the similar apps. They often pick the apps with highest rating stars.

You cannot bluntly users to rate your apps all the time with message. That will make users are unhappy. You have to have the dedicated way to ask them skillfully such as having it in setting area of your app, congruent notices, etc.

Nice ads in your app

You app is also a good place for you to put other appropriate and relevant ads. You can earn some good extra money with these ads without annoying your users.

The ads can appear in the free version of your ads. This will be a win win situation. Users will decide to upgrade the version to get rid of the ads. You earn money either way.

Video ads are good too. However, the videos should not be to long. You should select carefully the ads that will appear in your ads and also the ad networks. You always remember this is just a extra income. The main income stream is your priority app.

Chapter 7: Writing online reviews and passive income

You purchase different types of products online throughout the year. I think you leave reviews for the products or services at least couple times. Do you know that you can write online reviews and get paid? This is kind of a nice stream of income.

Writing skill for online reviews

Writing skill is very useful nowadays. You can just work at home. Your writing skill will earn you money. A lot of online businesses need people with good writing skill.

You can write the reviews for products, services and even brands to earn this income stream using your writing skill. You cannot just write anything random. It is real business, and you have to write honest reviews. The reviews may be positive or negative, and they are fine.

You can look for the review services. They will provide you work to write honest reviews. You will do some research to find what are good review services, tips to write a comprehensive reviews, etc.

Many potential customers first they search for what they want. Then they will look at the reviews on the products or services. The reviews are really important for both business and customers.

The reviews always must be honest. With the writing skill, you have to be careful for your word choice. Business will be harmful if you write fake reviews.

If you used the products or services, your reviews will be on point. You have a experience with it. The companies or business will pay you the reviews, and they may repay you the money that you purchased their products or services.

Get paid for writing reviews

Business and organizations want to pay good price for the service companies to get the reviews out there. Business will have a big chance for their products or services to reach to a lot of potential customers.

First, they reach potential customers. The potential customers will notice their products or services. The honest reviews weight in big time here.

Potential customers read reviews, and they will buy the products or services. The business will have the high conversion because of the honest reviews from writers.

As we see, writers will write honest reviews to receive the pay from service companies. Business win, service companies win and also the writers.

You should check to make sure the reviews service companies that are legit. They practice ethical business such as want honest reviews not fake reviews. The services also have established ways to pay the writers.

The services are in the field for a long time. They commit to the writers and business to provide value and legit reviews, not the get quick money methods.

You should concern about the services' niches. The services can focus on many niches, but the niches have to related at some points. This will show that the services commit with strong business model.

How to write precise reviews

In this part, I will show you some tips to write good and precise reviews. The reviews must always be honest. The reviews may be positive or negative, but they are honest reviews about the products or services.

In addition, the products or services are worth to introduce them to your love ones. When the products or services are trying to trick potential customers, you should not use the harsh languages to attack them.

Instead of that, you give the reason in full details why that you do not recommend these products or services. The potential customers will feel more appreciate towards your reviews.

The products or services that you used and had experiences with are way better. Your reviews will be all-inclusive. You will be like a relying expert to the potential customers. The paid rate of writing reviews will be better for you.

The outline of your reviews need to match the criteria that the potential customers are looking for. You have to practice your review writing skill before you start to write to earn money from reviews service companies.

Some of the popular reviews services companies right now are RateItAll, Review Stream, LinkFromBlog, etc. You can also do the research to find which services are fitting more with the writing niches that you are in.

Chapter 8: Get paid for lending money on credible platforms and passive income

This passive income stream is a little bit opposite with the writing reviews. This income stream is more towards the investment side. You have extra money, and you lend these extra money to earn good interest.

Peer to peer lending

The peer to peer lending is an interesting opportunity to earn passive income. Not a lot of investors mention about this, but it is worth to consider.

If you interest in peer to peer lending, you have to live in certain states that are allowing this business transaction. The level of income are in the equation as well. Different states require different level of income. You also need a legit bank account.

Prosper is one of the popular company for peer to peer lending. Proper can invest automatically for you. Lending Club is newer platform that compare to Prosper. Lending Club also has the automatic investment function. It means you can earn income even when you sleep.

Earn money by peer to peer lending

People will go to the crowd lending sites. You have extra money. You invest by lending your money for people that need it. You choose different types or portions of lending. Your earning is the interest.

You do not have to make $20,000 loan. You can choose how much portion that you want lend the money. You can choose to lend $1,000 or even just $100.

The other investors will contribute in different portions of the loan. When the loan is due, you will get your interest each month for the portion that you invest in. With certain amount of money, you can invest in many different loans.

Is any risk in peer to peer lending?

The potential risk is the people who loaned money do not want to repay for any reason. Any loan will have this potential risk. You will not completely avoid this risk.

However, in most case, people will do the best to pay back the loan with interest. Most people want to get the credibility because it will help for their future business loaning also.

Chapter 9: Get Paid to search and evaluate on the internet and passive income

Nowadays we search on the internet all the time. Our search skills are increasing day by day. I just want you to know that this stream of income is not totally passive income. However, it can bring you a nice stream of extra income.

Evaluating the search

You will make money by working at home in your comfy clothes. This stream is good for extra money. You will make potentially around $1,000 a month. You will evaluate these famous search engines such as Google, Bing, etc.

Search engines are working because of their algorithms. Each search engine will have different algorithm. For example, you type some words on the search box. Those words are keywords.

You will see also the suggestions for long tail keywords. When you press enter, the search engine will show hundred thousands or even million results.

These results are very related to your keywords searching. Search engine will execute within seconds to narrow the search results for users. You will see most related websites that will rank on first couple pages.

The search engines give the results quickly, so sometimes they will make big mistake as well. The mistakes are inevitable. Therefore, many real people are behind the scene to help fix the search engine right, and they also make it relevant to huge amount of internet users.

Is it worth a try?

You will become the evaluating person to these search engines. You will not their employee. You are the independent contractor. You will keep on what you work on yourself.

The companies will have you to sign the non-disclosure agreement. The search engine companies really pay attention in their algorithms and their privacy.

You will get an interview over the phone. You will have couple exams to do. The companies want to test to make sure that you are the right candidate for the job. The exam may take couple hours to finish as well.

This job has many advantages. You can take them to your consideration. You can work at home. You save a lot of time for transportation. You set your own schedule. This job is the extra income for you.

You will need to work certain minimum hours a month to still considering that you are the companies' independent contractors. You can decide to work minimum required hours or work more hours.

When you evaluate search engines, you will get more knowledge about many things. Search engines have a lot of topics that you did not even know are existing.

There are some companies that have this job available such as Leapforce, Lionbridge and other websites. This not a full time job. This is just an opportunity to earn some extra money to make your streams of income more stable.

Chapter 10: Cash back credit cards and passive income

Most people have their own credit cards. It is very convenient when you purchase goods or merchandises in person or of course online. You do not have to carry a lot of cash with you when you go out.

Most of us and credit cards

Is it interesting to know that you can also earn money with your credit cards? When I mention about credit card, most people will think immediately about the debt. It is just a natural thinking because most of us carried credit debts before for some different reasons.

When you have a credit card's debts, you do not only pay for the debt. You have to pay for interests and fees also. You need a good way to manage the spending in your credit card. If you do not manage well, you will waste your earning money.

You will need good plan of action to make the credit card works in your favors. You will not owe any debt, interest and fee. Your credit card will also give you good cash if you use it the right way.

Earning money with your credit cards

Some credit cards will give you cash back after you purchase stuff. Each credit card will have its own percent of cash back such as 1%, 3% or 5%. The percent depends on company, type of the card, and type of the purchasing products or services.

I will give general examples here. Your credit card will clearly state the percent cash back that you will receive. If you pay for gas, you will get 3% cash back.

If you shop for groceries, you will earn 1% cash back. If you pay for restaurants, you will get 5% cash back, etc. These are the clear examples that most of cash back credit cards work.

The cash back opportunity is interesting and worth to enroll. However, you must manage the way that you use the credit card in purchasing products or services. If you are not certain, you may got into debts instead of earn cash back.

Some credit cards will have bonus points to reward their users. The bonus points are often in the airplane traveling. The credit card will accumulate your flight mileage.

You can travel and earn those points. Later, the points will convert to cash. You will have expenses any way. These cards will be really good to pay for your expenses. It always good to earn some money back.

If you have big expenses, you can use your credit card to pay. Your credit card can pay rent, utilities, car and so much more. You will earn point for these payments.

Invest back the rewards

If you do not use the cash back, you can invest the cash to earn interest. This is very common and simple thing, and sometimes people completely forget about.

The interest will be compounding interests, so the money will grow quicker. You have your cash back. You do not spend it. You will find an reliable account that yields good percent of return. You put the money in that account and let's it grow.

You will have to search for the credit cards that match with your needs. The cards should not have many limitations. The card is good when it serve you full needs.

Chapter 11: Use your expertise and passive income

This is one of the ways that you can earn a decent amount of money when you want. You can sell your certain skills and expertise to create good stream of income.

The demand for your expertise

With the help of internet, it will be not difficult to find your good clients to offer your skills. Nowadays, the freelancing platforms are appearing more and more. You have many of options to choose.

If you are sill not sure about the demand or the market, there are a lot of market for freelancing. Business and organizations always need people to work on their certain tasks.

Platforms or sites to look for

There are many popular freelancing sites and platforms out there such as Guru, Upwork, Freelancer, Simply Hired, etc.

You do a little bit of search to these platforms, and you will see that your skills will work with these platforms or not. Most of the sites will accept multiple skills from different freelancers.

Different companies look for different skills. There are popular skills such as designing, accounting, writing, programming, editing, blogging, translating, etc. You will compete with other people for the job. You would at your skills, many job will be available.

Tips to earn money with your skill

You will put in details your information, your skills that you are really good at. You should tell more about your experience. These things are really helping when the organizations want to give the tasks to you.

You have to write a honest message on why you will finish the job for your clients. The message will be the guideline for the clients to know what you do with the job in certain steps.

You will take a deep look on the requirements. If you are not quite sure, you should ask the questions to clear things up right away. You want to complete the job in the good way.

You will always learn and grow with the constructive feedback from your clients. You should take note of that. You get the jobs that match with your skills, and you should always finish the job on time to earn the trust from your clients.

Conclusion

Thank you for making it through to the end of this book. I am feeling that you enjoy these good contents about what passive income is, passive income with blogging, graphic t-shirts design, trading cryptocurrency, selling your professional photos online, developing phone apps, writing online reviews, get paid for lending money on credible platforms, get paid to search and evaluate on the internet, cash back credit cards, and use your expertise. Again I really hope that the information in this book will be helpful for you.

www.ingramcontent.com/pod-product-compliance
Lightning Source LLC
Chambersburg PA
CBHW030055230526
45471CB00003B/1113